TO MY WONDERFUL GRAM

WHO ALWAYS TOOK
MY SIDE.

Published in the UK by Scholastic, 2024

1 London Bridge, London, SE1 9BG

Scholastic Ireland, 89E Lagan Road, Dublin Industrial Estate, Glasnevin, Dublin, D11 HP5F

SCHOLASTIC and associated logos are trademarks and/or
registered trademarks of Scholastic Inc.

Text and illustrations © Lewis Hancox, 2024

ISBN 978 0702 31450 6

A CIP catalogue record for this book is available from the British Library.

Printed in China by C&C Offset Printing Co,. Ltd.

Paper made from wood grown in sustainable forests and other controlled sources.

1 3 5 7 9 10 8 6 4 2

www.scholastic.co.uk

ESCAPE FROM ST. HELL

LOADING...

7TH SEPT 2008
AGE : 19
DAYS ON
TESTOSTERONE : 14

DAYS TIL I ESCAPE
ST. HELL : 9

2

4

5

7

8

PHEW, EMAIL'S STILL THERE.

Subject: Manchester Uni
From: manchesteruni@...com
To: sbeanlodge@...com

Dear Mr Hancox,
Congratulations! Your place at Manchester University to study Filmmaking has been confirmed.

OH CRUD. I'M DUE MY SHOT TODAY!

CAN'T HAVE **MUM** THINKING MY TESTOSTERONE LEVEL IS TOO HIGH, WHEN I NEED HER HELP **INJECTING** IT...

T
Sustanon 250mg

SORRY, MUM!

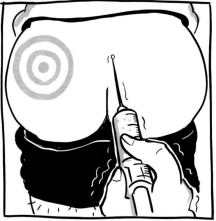

I HAD TO BATTLE A LOT OF BIG BOSSES TO GET ON TESTOSTERONE. I WAS LUCKY TO HAVE THESE SERVICES FOR FREE BUT IT TOOK **FOREVER**.

I GET THAT THE SYSTEM IS DESIGNED TO PROTECT YOU. BUT IT OFTEN FELT **OVERPROTECTIVE** AND LIKE I HAD TO CONSTANTLY PROVE MYSELF!

16

I FEEL LIKE ALL I'M DOING RIGHT NOW IS TRYING TO **NOT** LOOK LIKE A **GIRL** (CHECK MA **FLOORDROBE**)...

... AND **PRAYING** THAT I GROW SOME FACIAL HAIR!

CHARACTER SELECT

LEVEL ONE
THE LOOK

START ⊗

SO I WHACKED ON MY BINDER AND SET UPON MY MISSION.

I WAS SUDDENLY **HYPERAWARE** OF EVERY **GUY** AROUND ME.

SCRAWNY LIL SCALLY

I FEEL LIKE I'D NEED SOME BIG ALPHA ENERGY TO PULL THE CHAV LOOK OFF...

OF WHICH I HAVE **ZERO.**

SCANNING MAN STYLES

BIG BALD BEARDY BEAR

I'D QUITE LIKE A BIG MANLY BELLY...
BUT KNOWING MY BOD, ALL THE FAT WOULD GO STRAIGHT TO MA BOOBS!

WITHOUT A BEARD I'D LOOK LIKE AN EGGHEAD.

TALL SKINNY SCENE KID

YEAH, I'M 5'4"... MAYBE NOT.

SLICK SUITED ESTATE AGENT GENT

I WONDER WHAT IT FEELS LIKE TO WEAR A SUIT... WOULD IT FIT MY STUPID BODY SHAPE??

I'VE YET TO TRY HAIR GEL. I NORMALLY JUST USE MUM'S HAIRSPRAY!

café Geek Retreat Games

TO LET

LONG-HAIRED DUNGEONS & DRAGONS DUDE

LONG HAIR WOULD MAKE ME FEEL WAY TOO MUCH LIKE "LOIS."

I'VE NEVER PLAYED A ROLE PLAYING GAME... UNLESS YOU COUNT PLAYING THE ROLE OF A GIRL FOR 18 YEARS OF MA LIFE.

25

I GREW UP **SKATEBOARDING** SO I'D SURELY FIND MY LOOK HERE!

SKATING HELPED ME FEEL LIKE ONE OF THE **BOYS** ON MY BLOCK.

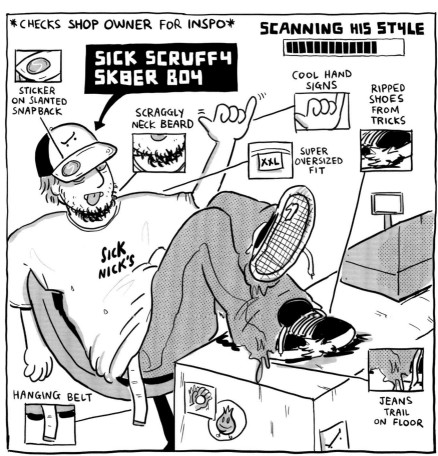

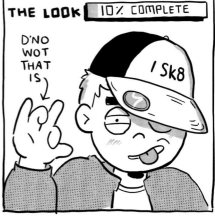

31

I DITCHED SKATING AND FOCUSED BACK ON MY GYM ROUTINE.

I DECIDED TO TRY LOOKING LESS **SKATER** AND MORE **SPORTY**.

OBSERVING GUYS FROM **AFAR** WAS A RUNNING THEME IN MY LIFE...

WELL, I WAS **DONE** JUST OBSERVING. I WAS GONNA BE A **BRO**.

37

I NEEDED TO SEE ME MATES TO CALM DOWN. WE WENT TO A GIG IN TOWN. I'D ONLY EVER GOTTEN READY WITH THE GIRLS. WHAT DID **DUDES** DO?

I BECAME FIXATED ON THE **PUNK** KINDA VIBE.

CAN I GET MY EARS STRETCHED, PLEASE?

IT'S A LONG PROCESS.

URGH, BUT I WANT IT NOW!!!

KCHUNK

GOTTA START SOMEWHERE, I GUESS.

THE LOOK `1% COMPLETE`

I TURNED TO MUM FOR SOME HELP...

MUMMM, THERE'S A SUIT ONLINE I REALLY NEEEEED BUT I'VE NOT GOT ENOUGH MONEY–

OH, LEW, I'M NOT YER RUDDY CASH POINT!

CHRIS'LL BRING YOU ONE OF HIS OLD SUITS.

WILL I?

I WAS STILL ADJUSTING TO MUM HAVING A BOYFRIEND.

EW, NO. IT WON'T BE THE RIGHT STYLE.

EY, I'M **FUNKY** AS THEY COME, ME!

TELL HIM, LYNNE!

NEXT DAY:

'ERE YOU ARE, LEW.

OK, IT'S NOT AWFUL.

BET YER MUM WOULD GO MAD FOR ME IN THIS IF IT STILL FIT.

YUCK!!!

THE LOOK | 11% COMPLETE

MUM'S HAIRSPRAY

PSSH

HAIRSPRAY

THE LOOK | 21% COMPLETE

OLD PIN BADGES FROM THE DEPTHS OF MA DRAWERS.

blink 182

TEGAN AND SARA

URGH, THIS IS GIVING ME THE GENDER DYSPHORIA BLUES!!

MY HAIRLINE IS SO FAR FORWARDS I.E. FEMININE.

TOO WIDE ON SHOULDERS.

I'M JUST NOT BUILT LIKE OTHER MEN.

TIGHT IN THE WRONG PLACES.

BINDER SHOWS THROUGH SHIRT.

TOO LONG ON MY T.REX ARMS.

SOMETIMES I'D WONDER WHY I WAS **BOTHERING** TO STYLE MYSELF...

OR WHY I WAS SO **STRICT** WITH MY WORKING OUT AND PROTEIN DIET.

THERE WERE BITS OF MY BODY EVEN **TESTOSTERONE** COULDN'T FIX.

THE LOOK

0% COMPLETE

I ENDED UP CONFIDING IN JESS, MY BESTIE SINCE FOREVER.

I HONESTLY DREADED THAT I WOULDN'T HAVE JESS AROUND WHEN I WAS AT UNI. SHE WAS MY GUIDE TO LIFE AND LOWKEY LOWERED MY

I'M KINDA SURPRISED JESS WOULD GO FOR A GUY LIKE GUS. HE'S NOT EXACTLY YOUR **TYPICAL** MAN. GIVES ME SOME HOPE!

I LIKE YOUR JUMPER, BTW!

OH, THANKS, DUDE.

IT'S 100% ORGANIC WOOL. SO SOFT.

GOT IT FROM THIS MEN'S SHOP IN TOWN.

I GET ALL MY RAD GARMS FROM THERE.

OMG, YOU TWO SHOULD SO GO **SHOPPING** TOGETHER!!!

I'M DOWN, MAN.

I'M DOWN TOO, ER, **MOOD!**

...

OH, ERM, I WENT TO SAY MAN THEN SWITCHED TO **DUDE**... HEH...

OK, GUS WAS A BIT PRETENTIOUS BUT IT FELT DEAD GOOD HAVING A MALE FRIEND! I THINK HE ENJOYED PLAYING BIG BROTHER TO ME.

IS IT BETRAYING JESS IF I TALK ABOUT HER?

BUT I THINK I'VE FINALLY FOUND SOMEONE TO HAVE MAN TALK WITH!

JESS IS PROPER INTO YOU. SHE TELLS ME EVERYTHING.

COOL, THANKS, MAN.

I'VE HAD A RAD TIME TODAY.

3 FOR 2

MAN CREAM

BEARD WASH

BEARD OIL

MAN SCENT

IT'S NOT LIKE I WANTED TO **BE** GUS... I JUST THOUGHT HE WAS **RAD**.

LATERS, DUDE!

BYE, MAN!

Pound Shop

BACON BUTTY £1.50

OPEN

£1

£1

Every item ★ £1 ★

Reading Glasses £1

THE LOOK 30% COMPLETE

ONE LAST NIGHT OUT WITH THE WHOLE GANG AT THE LOCAL HAUNTS.

BAR JAVA

ERM, I SAID GO SHOPPING, NOT MERGE INTO ONE.

IPA

I THINK YOU LOOK RAD, DUDE.

HAHA. TA, MAN.

LEW, I'LL BE AT THE BAR WHEN YOU'RE DONE GIGGLING WITH GUS.

IPA

EVEN WITH MY NEW LOOK I WAS STILL GETTING BLOODY MISGENDERED!

THE FACT ALL MA BESTIES WERE **GIRLS** PROBS DIDN'T HELP MY CASE.

DRINKS WON'T BE THIS CHEAP IN MANCHESTER.

AT LEAST I'M NOT MOVING TO LONDON LIKE ALISON!

WANNA BE AS FAR AS POSS FROM ST. HELL.

GUS, HUN, GO AWAY FOR A BIT, WE WANT SOME GIRL TIME.

GIRL TIME

IPA

ERR, **JESS!**

WHIP

SHIT, SORRY, LEW. I WAS JUST GETTIN' ALL EMOSH... I DIDN'T MEAN ANYTHIN' BY IT!

AWKWARD

MAYBE I WOULD MISS THIS TOWN A LIL TINY BIT.

THERE WAS ONE FINAL STOP TO MAKE...

WE WEREN'T READY TO LEAVE EACH OTHER, SO WE HEADED TO THE PARK.

ME AND JESS FINALLY HEADED HOME AT 4 AM.

LEW, I LOVE YOU, BUT YOU'RE SO STUPID.

WHAT?! WHY??

YOU'RE TRYING SOOO HARD TO CHANGE YOUR IMAGE...

YOU'RE BEING SOMEONE YOU'RE NOT.

YOU WERE JUST FINE BEFORE!

REALLY, JESS? YA SURE??

YES, NOW DON'T ASK ME A MILLION TIMES.

YOU BETTER NOT FORGET ABOUT ME WHEN YOU'RE OFF IN THE BIG CITY, BIATCH.

HUG

OBVS I WON'T. BIATCH.

I FELT LIKE I'D BECOME A MIX OF ALL DIFFERENT KINDS OF MEN...

LUCKILY, DAD RAN A LIL LAUNDERETTE IN TOWN.

IT GAVE ME A CHANCE FOR SOME "MAN TIME" BEFORE I LEFT.

MEN ARE ALWAYS MADE OUT TO BE LESS SENSITIVE BUT I HADN'T GIVEN IT MUCH THOUGHT BEFORE. DAD'S COMMENT SPUN ROUND AND ROUND IN MY BRAIN.

ONE THING WAS CLEAR... DAD DEFO DIDN'T WANNA DEAL WITH HIS FEELINGS ABOUT MY TRANSITION.

LEVEL TWO
EMOTIONS
CONTINUE

It's funny how I clung on to certain items like I didn't have a personality without them.

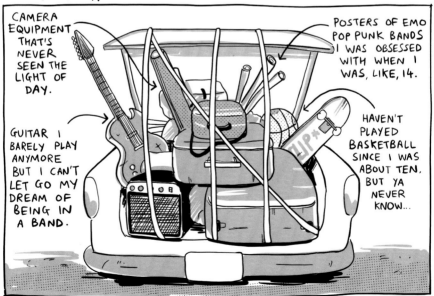

MUM AND DAD HAD BEEN SPLIT EIGHT YEARS. ON RARE OCCASIONS WHEN WE WERE ALL TOGETHER, I FELT LIKE A **CHILD** AGAIN.

I COULD FEEL MY EMOTIONS RISING, AND BEFORE I EVEN HAD TIME TO THINK ABOUT HOW TO HANDLE THEM...

I RETURNED TO **"START."**

NO GOING BACK NOW...

I HAD A ONE WAY TICKET TO:

OK, IT'S ONLY LIKE A 30-MIN DRIVE AWAY, BUT STILL...

IT'S A MILLION MILES FROM MA MISERABLE HOMETOWN.

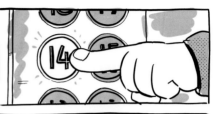

NEW DESTINATION UNLOCKED: STUDENT FLAT

I COULD SEE MELKA'S EYES TRYING TO SUSS ME OUT...
I IMAGINED HER THINKING...

BUT SHE DIDN'T SAY ANYTHING, SHE JUST TOOK ME UNDER HER WING.

AS WE WERE SHOPPING, MELKA MADE ME AWARE OF JUST HOW DIFFERENT MEN'S AND WOMEN'S STUFF WAS MARKETED. I HADN'T REALLY NOTICED...

WOMEN'S WERE ABOUT **SHAME**...

MEN'S WERE ABOUT **POWER**!

(I WAS ON A NEW HIGH-PROTEIN MEAL PLAN I'D FOUND IN A BODY-BUILDING FORUM. IT REQUIRED LITTLE COOKING SKILL.)

FUNNY HOW I ALWAYS FOUND MYSELF IN THE LESBIAN SCENE. TRUTH IS, I'D ALWAYS FELT AT **HOME** THERE.

BUT NOW THAT I WANTED TO BE SEEN AS A **GUY**, WAS I A PRETENDER IN **PLAID**?

THIS WAS MY FIRST CHANCE TO FIT IN WITH NEW FRIENDS. THE MORE ACCEPTED I FELT, THE HARDER IT BECAME TO REVEAL THE REAL ME!

APPARENTLY I'D GONE FROM LOIS TO LEWIS TO LOUISE...

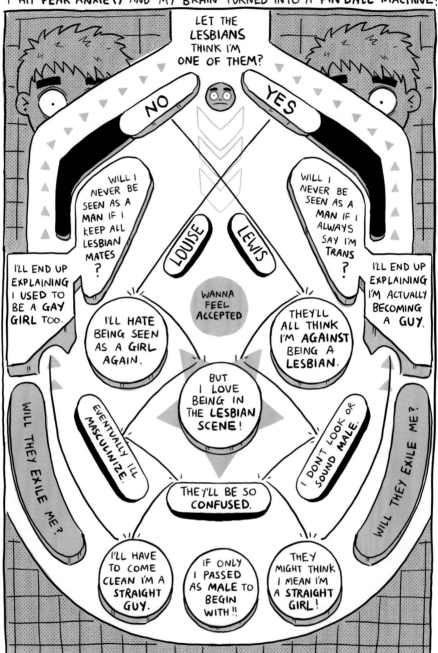

THE OTHERS ALL HEADED OUT TO CANAL STREET. I DIDN'T JOIN.

I WAS STILL GRAPPLING WITH WHETHER I BELONGED IN THAT WORLD. I TORTURED MYSELF OVER HOW I'D HANDLED THINGS AT THE PARTY.

URGH, WHY DOES MY MOUTH ALWAYS HAVE TO RUN AWAY WITH ITSELF?

WASN'T VERY MANLY TO OVERSHARE LIKE THAT.

I FEEL SO STUPID.

WISH I COULD DO WHAT MEN DO AND LAUGH IT OFF

FRESHERS WEEK WAS FINALLY OVER. I ALMOST FORGOT THE ACTUAL
REASON I'D MOVED HERE... UNI.

THANKFULLY THE CLASSES WERE SO BIG I FELT PRETTY ANONYMOUS.

AS I HEADED BACK TO MY UNI FLAT, I KEPT THINKING ABOUT MY FIRST ASSIGNMENT.
COCKTAILS
APART FROM TRANSITIONING, WHAT EVEN IS THERE ABOUT ME?
YOU'D THINK SOMEONE WITH MAIN CHARACTER SYNDROME WOULD FIND THIS EASIER.
Practical Filmmaking Class
Video portrait
about ME?
I DON'T DO ANY OF THE THINGS I USED TO LOVE...
Video portra
about ME?
COMIC
Video portrait
about ME?
I CAN'T EVEN DRAW ANYMORE!!!
SCRUNCH

I GOT MY CAMERA STUFF OUT AND DECIDED TO JUST GO FOR IT. (IT WAS GONNA BE CRAP ANYWAY.)

HEY, GUYS, IT'S LEWIS...

I'M A TRANSGENDER GUY...

I'VE BEEN ON TESTOSTERONE FOR 40 DAYS NOW...

BUT I'VE NOT HAD ANY **CHANGES** YET, ANNOYINGLY...

THAT'LL DO FOR NOW.

BLEEP

WAIT...

WHAT!

1 CHIN HAIR.

MY DAYS STARTED TO REVOLVE AROUND WORKING ON MY BOD...

FOLLOWING MY FREAKY FOOD PLAN DOWN TO A T...

AND DOCUMENTING MY CHANGES, WHICH WERE FINALLY HAPPENING!

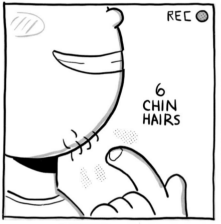

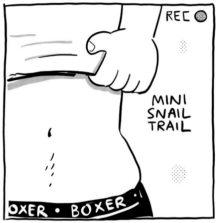

MY HARDCORE REGIME KINDA **ISOLATED** ME...

WANNA COME OUT TO CANAL STREET, LEWIS?

SORRY, I GOTTA COOK PROTEIN MEAL #3!

EW, NOT YOUR STINKY TUNA FISH BROTH AGAIN!?!

I'LL COME NEXT TIME!

YEAH YEAH.

I JUST CAN'T LOSE CONTROL. Oₒₒ

I KNEW I WAS DAMAGING MY HEALTH AND FALLING BACK INTO OLD HABITS:

HOW COULD YOU MISS MA BDAY PARTY, LOIS?!

SO SOZ, JESS, I WAS BUSY!

YOU ALWAYS ARE. I'M DONE.

(BUSY = TRYING TO BURN MY CURVES OFF ON MUM'S CROSSTRAINER)

104

I THINK IT DROVE A WEDGE BETWEEN ME AND MY FLATMATES.

NOT-SO-FUN GAME - FIND ALL 14 TUNA CANS BEFORE I BECOME SKIN AND BONE!!!!

106

MELKA FORCED ME OUTA MY ROUTINE AND INTO THE CITY CENTRE FOR A MOOCH.

I WAS EXCITED TO MEASURE MY STRENGTH ON THE PUNCH BAG MACHINE.

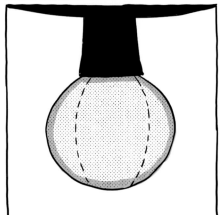

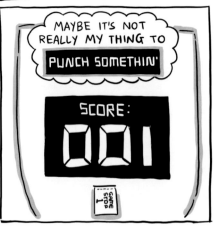

WE LEFT WITH THE ONLY SHITTY PRIZE WE COULD AFFORD.

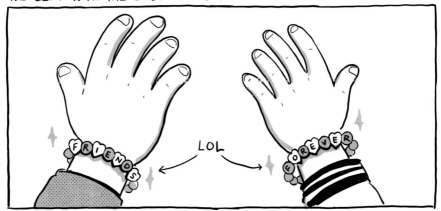

AND ENDED UP HAVIN' SOME BEVVIES ON CANAL STREET.

I UPDATED THEM ON EVERYTHING WHILE WE KNOCKED AROUND TOWN, WAITING FOR THE CLUBS TO OPEN.

UNEXPECTEDLY, IT LED TO MY FIRST "LADS NIGHT".

IT WAS HARD NOT TO FEEL LIKE AN IMPOSTER.

MAN TALK

MAN TALK

MY DIRTY LIL SECRET COCKTAIL →

LOOK AT THEM TALKING ABOUT RANDOM STUFF...

BLAH

BLAH DREAM CAR...

BLAH

BLAH THIS BAND...

BLAH

...ANYTHING BUT THEIR FEELINGS.

BLAH NEW GAME...

NEW ALBUM...

BLAH

BLAH

WOLF WHISTLE CHECK OUT THE FITTIES!

GAH! I REMEMBER HOW IT FELT TO BE CAT-CALLED...

118

I WAS IN MY "GIRLY FITTING IN" PHASE. I FELT SO VIOLATED. I SWORE I'D NEVER BE THAT KINDA GUY.

USING THE MEN'S PUB TOILETS WAS QUITE A MANHOOD MILESTONE.

I FOUND JESS IN A PRECARIOUS SITUATION...

OI, GIVE ME MA PHONE BACK, DICKHEAD!

NOT UNTIL MY NUMBER'S IN IT, DARLIN'!

OH SHIT, JESS IS IN TROUBLE!

MY WHOLE LIFE IT'S ALWAYS BEEN JESS SAVING ME...

IS IT MY TURN TO SAVE HER?

OR IS IT WANKY TO ASSUME SHE CAN'T SAVE HERSELF?

PUSH

ARGH!

I CAN'T JUST STAND BY AND NOT HELP!!

EY!!

GET OFF HER!!

123

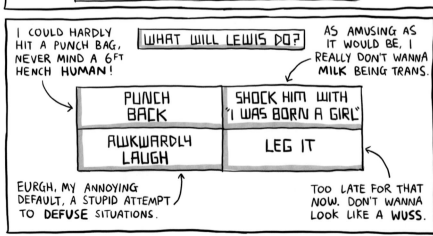

I FELT LIKE EVERYBODY WANTED ME TO STAY THE SAME.

THERE WAS AN IMPORTANT MESSAGE I'D BEEN PUTTING OFF OPENING...

To: L3W15_89
FROM: MELKA
SUBJECT: Yo!

Lew, I think I mistook our friendship for more. Honestly you're awesome and we connect so well which is why I got a bit confused. I hope we can continue being friends. xx

I REPLIED TO MELKA A MILLION TIMES IN MY **HEAD** ON THE TRAIN...

I KNEW I COULDN'T AVOID EVERYONE FOREVER... BUT I COULD TRY.

THINGS WITH MELKA TURNED OUT TO BE TOTALLY CHILL...

..BUT IT DID LEAVE A LOT OF TABS OPEN IN MY BRAIN.

LEVEL THREE
LOVE LIFE
CONTINUE

I LOOKED THROUGH MY MEMENTO BOX AND THOUGHT ABOUT WHAT I COULD LEARN FROM MY DISASTROUS DATING HISTORY.

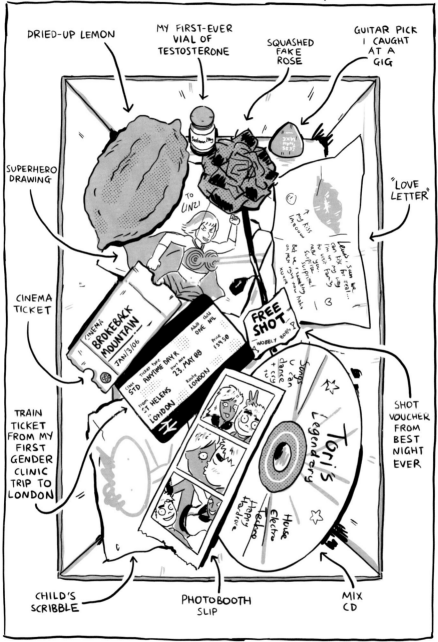

143

DRIED-UP LEMON →

I MET POLLY AT A GIG...

FROSTED LEMON COWARD...

TEGAN AND SARA

18-YR-OLD ME →

OMFG YOU LOOK LIKE SARA!

ME?? NOOO..

YOU SO DO!

AFTER THE GIG:

WHAT SHOULD I SAVE YOU AS?

ERM... JUST "L".

TAP TAP

TAP TAP

I WAS STILL TESTING THE WATERS WITH MY MALE IDENTITY.

DATE #1:

WHY DOES YOUR MYSPACE BIO SAY "KING OF CRINGE"?

COZ I'M AWKS AF.

NO, I MEAN, SHOULDN'T IT BE QUEEN?

OH! I DUNNO. MAYBE.

CHEAP BOOZE

CHEAP BOOZE

I LIKED POLLY A LOT BUT SHE CLEARLY LIKED ME AS A **GIRL**.

DATE #2:

I BROUGHT YOU A GIFT TO REMIND YOU OF WHEN WE MET.

ITEM COLLECTED: LEMON

to a special girl

THE MORE **WRONG** IT FELT, THE MORE IT **CONFIRMED** WHO I WAS...

DATE #3:

ALL WOMEN POSTERS IN POLLY'S ROOM

KISS

WOULD YOU STILL FANCY ME IF I WAS A **GUY**?

LET'S JUST SAY I'M GLAD YOU'RE NOT.

WE TALKED ABOUT IT AND THINGS TURNED PRETTY **SOUR**.

BUT I'D BE THE SAME, JUST MORE MASCULINE...

I JUST CAN'T IMAGINE IT!

AM I NOT BOYISH ALREADY THEN?

I'M 100% A GUY.

I'M 100% GAY.

LESSON #1: BE WITH SOMEONE WHO SEES ME AS A GUY TO BEGIN WITH.

145

MIX CD ↓

Tori's Legendary

House Electro Techno Happy hardcore

Songs u can dance + cry to

MIX

TORI WAS JUST A MATE...

MUM'S AWAY, I'M HAVIN' A PARTY!

I'LL PROVIDE THE CHOONS!

A MATE I'D OCCASIONALLY GET OFF WITH AT PARTIES.

♪ SHOW ME LOVE ♪

IT'S OUR SONG!

SNOG

HERE WE GO AGAIN...

I THINK IT MEANT MORE TO ME THAN IT DID TO HER.

♪ YOU'VE BEEN CHEATIN' A

ND TELLIN' ME LIES ♪

OUR SITUATIONSHIP CAME TO AN END IN A DRUNKEN ROW.

I PUSHED TOO HARD AND GOT AN ANSWER THAT CRUSHED ME.

IT MAY HAVE JUST BEEN AN EXCUSE BUT I'LL NEVER KNOW.

LESSON #2: NOT EVERYONE IS GONNA BE OK WITH DATING A TRANS PERSON.

THERE WAS JADE, WHO WAS A YOUNG MUM. SHE MAINLY LIKED GIRLS, WITH THE ODD "EXCEPTION" (I HOPED I CLASSED AS ONE)...

BUT I WAS BARELY CONFIDENT LIVING AS A "MAN" YET, NEVER MIND A "FAMILY MAN"!

> DADDA!

> NOT READY.

ITEM COLLECTED: CHILD'S SCRIBBLE

LESSON #3: FIND SOMEONE AT THE SAME LIFE STAGE AS ME.

THEN THERE WAS PICKLE, WHO BINNED ME AFTER ONE DATE. I LATER FOUND HER SECRET BLOG THAT MADE IT CLEAR I WAS JUST A TICK ON HER

PHOTOBOOTH

Four Poses Only £4

> LET'S KISS ON THIS ONE!

BUCKET LIST
- ☑ Get with a ♥ girl ♥ 👄
- ☑ See 🎵 Enter Shikari 🎵
- ☑ Go on a date with a transgender (receipt) →
- ☐ Bungee jump 0-0
- ☐ Marry a man

ITEM COLLECTED: PHOTOBOOTH SLIP

LESSON #4: I DON'T WANNA BE SOMEONE'S NOVELTY.

THEN THERE WAS GARY. AFTER I STARTED GOING BY "LEWIS" HE TOLD ME HE FANCIED ME! ON GAY NIGHT IN TOWN WE HAD A SNOG!!! I WAS DRAWN IN BY HIS ATTENTION BUT IT REALLY DIDN'T FEEL RIGHT.

LESSON #5: DON'T GET FLATTERED SO EASILY!

THEN THERE WAS FIFI, A PENPAL OF SORTS. I WASN'T ON MY TESTOSTERONE YET AND I DIDN'T BOTHER TO TELL HER I WAS TRANS SINCE SHE LIVED IN IRELAND SO NO CHANCE OF MEETING IRL... UNTIL...

I ENDED UP BEING THE ASSHOLE AND GHOSTING HER.

LESSON #6: NOT BEING **REAL** WITH PEOPLE HAS CONSEQUENCES.

NOW I WAS THIRSTY FOR A FRESH START, TO MEET SOMEONE AS THIS ME.

I POSTED A CRINGEY, COPY N' PASTED, NOT-SO-SUBTLE QUIZ TO THE MYSPACE BULLETIN BOARD. (THERE WERE LIMITED WAYS TO PUT YOURSELF OUT THERE IN 2008.)

A FEW HOURS LATER, I GOT A REPLY!

DID I JUST GET MY FIRST POTENTIAL BOYFRIEND POINT?

To: L3W15_89
From: Rockabilly-Rae
Subject: RE: ROMANCE Q

Bonjour!
I love your date idea omggg.
PS I'm only 5'2" ☺

BF +1

YOU COULD TELL A LOT ABOUT SOMEONE FROM THEIR **MYSPACE** PROFILE.

CAT LOVER (ME TOO!)

LIVES IN MY COMFORT ZONE

HER PROFILE SONG IS FROM MY FAVE FILM "JUNO"

www.myspace.com

Rockabilly-Rae
F 19 St.Hell

myspace

Anyone Else But You
THE MOLDY PEACHES

GOOD AT HTML CODING - SHE'S CLEVER AND CREATIVE

About Me:

☑ Msg   ☑ Forward
🔍 Add   ☑ Faves
🔍 Instant Msg   ✕ Block
➕ Group   ↑ Rank

I rewind movies for a living lolz <3

Rockabilly-Rae's Friends:

Status: Single
Sexuality: Straight
Zodiac: Virgo

INTO GUYS ONLY.

NO MUTUAL FRIENDS WITH ME - SHE DOESN'T KNOW MY **HISTORY**

SOUNDS LIKE A MINT JOB

75% COMPATIBILITY RATING WITH GEMINI (ME)

OVER THE NEXT MONTH I'D CAREFULLY CRAFT EVERY MESSAGE TO RAE,
CREATING MY "PERFECT" ONLINE PERSONA AND ANALYZING EVERYTHING.

I WANTED TO TELL RAE **IRL**, SO WHEN I GOT BACK TO MY ROOM I SPENT ALL NIGHT PERFECTING THIS SIMPLE MESSAGE:

Rockabilly_Rae:
It's a date! :)

Rockabilly_Rae:
My number-
079335354 X

IS IT THOUGH?

+5 BF

WONDER IF GUS WOULD APPROVE OF MY FIT.

GUS SAID EVERY MAN NEEDS A SIGNATURE SCENT.

UNISEX COLOGNE MUM BOUGHT ME WHEN I FIRST CAME OUT AS TRANS.

SPRITZ

cK one

I READ SOME-WHERE HOT LEMON TEA RELAXES YOUR VOCAL CORDS TO HELP YOUR VOICE SOUND DEEPER.

SLURP

WISH I COULD ASK **JESS** FOR SOME DATE ADVICE BUT I THINK SHE HATES ME...

LITTLE DID I KNOW:

WISH I COULD TELL **LEW** ME AND GUS BROKE UP BUT I THINK HE HATES ME...

ME AND RAE PLANNED TO MEET UP AT MANCHESTER'S CHRISTMAS MARKET.

IT WAS EITHER THE COLD OR MY NERVES GIVING ME THE SHAKES.

OMG, SHE LOOKS EVEN BETTER THAN HER PICTURES!

BONJOUR.

I HOPE I LOOK LIKE MINE.

HIYA.

I TRIED TO BE WHAT I **THOUGHT** WAS THE **BEST POSSIBLE VERSION** OF ME.

AFTER THAT WE GRABBED A DRINK.

OH CRUD. TURNS OUT I WON'T GET THIS...

BUT IT WAS IMPOSSIBLE TO NOT WORRY ABOUT EVERY LITTLE THING!

I WONDERED IF AND WHEN THE "RIGHT TIME" WOULD COME...

I WANTED TO KISS HER GOODBYE BUT DIDN'T KNOW IF I SHOULD.

I'VE HAD A LOVELY DAY.

↑ "DAY" OR "DATE"?

DITTO.

MEN ALWAYS MAKE THE FIRST MOVE IN THE MOVIES...

...BUT I DON'T WANNA COME ACROSS FORCEFUL...

I COULD ASK FOR A KISS BUT THAT SOUNDS LOSER-ISH.

AU REVOIR!

SEE YA.

BACK IN HALLS:

I WERE TOO SCARED TO KISS HER, NOW I'M REALLY GONNA MISS HER,

MAYBE IT'S FOR THE BETTER THOUGH, COZ IF I EVER LET HER KNOW,

I'M NOT WHAT SHE THOUGHT,

SHE'D BE PROPER DISTRAUGHT...

LEW, ME EARS CAN'T TAKE IT!

JUST WHEN I WAS STARTING TO ENJOY MY HEARTBREAK...

PING

Rockabilly Rae:

Really wish I'd kissed you >_<

+5 BF

NO WAY!!! SHIIIT, NOW I HAVE TO TELL HER... URGH, 'ERE I GO...

Rae...

Oui?

TAP TAP TAP

I really do have to tell you summat...

What???

So sorry about this...

Pls don't judge me...

Stop leaving me on a cliff hanger !!!

RAE HAD A LOT OF QUESTIONS, NATURALLY. I FOUND THAT THE MORE **OPEN** I WAS ABOUT STUFF, THE MORE AT **EASE** WE BOTH SEEMED TO BE.

A FEW DAYS LATER I TREKKED TO ST. HELL TO SURPRISE RAE AT WORK.

I BOUGHT HER A MEAL DEAL.

YOU SAID YOU NEVER GET TIME TO GRAB LUNCH SO... SORRY IF I'M BEIN' CRINGEY...

CUTE!

PECK

BF +5

I'VE GOT SUMMAT FOR YOU... AN OLD FILM ABOUT A TRANS MAN. IT'S A MASTERPIECE.

A MEMENTO!

BOYS DON'T CRY

ITEM COLLECTED: VHS

I STILL FELT ON EDGE, LIKE I COULD LOSE ALL MY POTENTIAL BOYF POINTS AT ANY MOMENT.

MUM HAD DROPPED A BIT OF A **BOMBSHELL** ON ME EARLIER...

WE TOOK ADVANTAGE OF RAE'S FREE HOUSE.

I LET GO OF MY BODYBUILDING DIET FOR ONE NIGHT SO I DIDN'T LOOK TOO WEIRD.

HORROR FILM SO SHE'D HOPEFULLY CUDDLE ME IN FEAR.

A TENTATIVE ARM

N'YAAAAH!!

BOOM

JUMP

HEH...

KISS

+10 BF

PSTTT...

BACK IN UNI HALLS:

MELKA, COME LOOK!

I'D DEVELOPED THIS TOXIC TRAIT OF MYSPACE STALKING RAE'S **EX**.

HOW AM I SUPPOSED TO COMPETE WITH THIS?!

BigmanDan_88
Photos

LOOK AT HIM SO CAREFREE. I BET RAE LOVED HIS CONFIDENCE.

HE'S 6'3"! I KNOW COZ I COUNTED THE HOUSE BRICKS BESIDE HIM...

HE ROCKS HIS DADBOD!

I WOULDN'T BOTHER WITH THE GYM EITHER IF I WAS BORN A GUY...

AND WORST OF ALL, HE'S GOT SUMMAT I TOTALLY LACK! ONE MASSIVE...

CHIN!!!

I KEPT FALLING DOWN THE SAME MANHOLE OF HANGUPS...

IT TOOK ALL MY STRENGTH TO PULL MYSELF OUT AND RETURN TO

REAL LIFE WAS EQUALLY AS SCARY...

THE LAST THING I WANTED WAS A BOLLOCKING BY MY TUTOR BUT THE ALTERNATIVE OF GETTING KICKED OUT OF UNI AND LIVING BACK AT MUM'S SEEMED WAY WORSE.

I CRINGED AS I PLAYED HER MY TRANSITION MONTAGE.

IT DAWNED ON ME I WAS PLAYING THE **UNCUT**, OVERLY PERSONAL EDIT!

OOPS, WAIT, THIS IS—

EVEN MA BUM'S GETTIN' HAIRY NOW...

OUTSTANDING! COURAGEOUS! THOUGHT-PROVOKING!

I LOOK FORWARD TO SEEING THE FINAL FILM ON SCREENING DAY.

REALLY?! NO WAY, DO YOU ACTUALLY THINK IT'S GOOD?

NOW, MR. HANCOX, I UNDERSTAND YOU HAVE A **LOT** GOING ON IN YOUR PERSONAL LIFE...

WE OFFER MENTAL HEALTH SUPPORT HERE AT THE UNI...

THERAPY FOR STUDENTS

NOW AVAILABLE AT MANCHESTER UNIVERSITY

Cleaner Wanted Apply now

LGBT GROUP MEET UP

JOBS - CAT FOOD TESTER

DRAMA CLASS

FILM OFFICE

HMMM... I HATED THE COUNSELLING I HAD BACK IN HIGH SCHOOL..

BUT I REMEMBER GUS SAID THERAPY HELPED HIM...

MAYBE I'LL TRY AGAIN SOMEDAY.

MEANWHIILE I STILL HAD TO FIGURE OUT WHAT I WAS DOING WITH RAE. WE'D HAD 5 DATES, BUT I WAS STILL TERRIFIED TO PUT A FOOT WRONG.

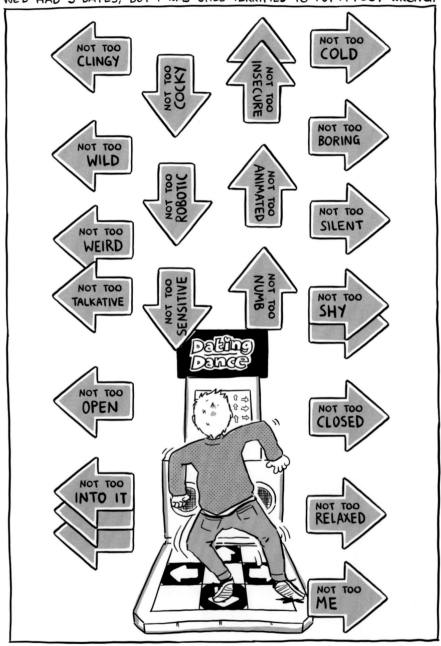

FACING THINGS HEAD-ON WAS MY NEW ENDEAVOR...

I INVITED RAE TO MY UNI HALLS OVER THE WEEKEND. IT WAS COOL SEEING HER AND MELKA VIBIN', MY WORLDS COLLIDING.

THAT WAS THE FIRST TIME I REALLY FELT LIKE A BOYFRIEND.

MY SUPERPOWER WAS TURNING GOOD THINGS INTO MORE ANXIETIES.

I TOLD MUM **NOT** TO MAKE A **FUSS** WHEN SHE METS RAE.

MUM AND RAE GOT ON SO WELL! MAYBE A LITTLE **TOO WELL**...

WHEN RAE NIPPED TO THE BATHROOM, I GAVE MUM AN EARFUL.

I MET RAE'S **DAD** (AKA MUM'S BOSS) AT THEIR FAMILY BARBECUE. I WAS DESPERATE TO MAKE A GOOD IMPRESSION.

I LOVED HOW RAE MADE ME FEEL LIKE JUST A REGULAR GUY. NOT THAT I WAS VERY REGULAR...

WHAT SNACKS SHOULD WE GET FOR MOVIE NIGHT?

ERM, PROTEIN BALLS?

CRUD, I NEED TO SNEAK THESE IN THE TROLLEY SOMEHOW!

YEAH, I'M THINKING MORE LIKE TORTILLA CHIPS.

SOUNDS GOOD.

TOSS

ERM, BABE, DID YOU PUT THAT IN HERE? BAHAHAHAHA, WHY THE HELL WOULD YOU NEED—

(WAIT FOR IT...)

CRISPS PADS

SINKS IN

OH HH HH HH HH HH HH!

IT'S FUNNY, I JUST TOTALLY FORGET THAT YOU'RE TRANS!

GROCERY STORE

I WISHED I HAD THE LUXURY OF FORGETTING I WAS TRANS.

I COULD ONLY DREAM OF WHAT IT'D BE LIKE TO HAVE HER LIE ON MY BARE CHEST.

PROGRESS ON MY QUEST FOR CHEST SURGERY WAS DEAD SLOW.

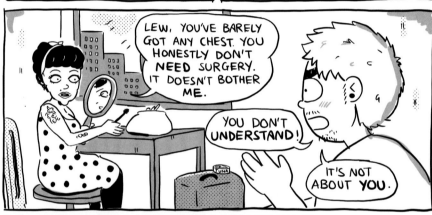

ME N' RAE GOT INTO SOME STUPID ROW.

IT MADE ME STEP BACK AND REEVALUATE OUR RELATIONSHIP.

IT WAS MY HOMETOWN BESTIE I NEEDED TO ANXIETY VOMIT TO.

I SENT JESS AN ESSAY...

OR AT LEAST I THOUGHT I DID...

MELKA DID ME A SOLID AND DROVE ME TO RAE'S WORK PRONTO.

I FELT THAT **OVERTALKING** ABOUT IT WITH MY MATES COULD SOMEHOW CHANGE THE OUTCOME.

I'M JUST REALLY WORRIED THAT I'LL NEVER **FIND ANYONE AGAIN**, RAE WAS SUCH A RARITY, SHE WAS EXCLUSIVELY INTO GUYS AND DIDN'T CARE THAT I WAS DIFFERENT, I SHOULD'VE **APPRECIATED** HER MORE, I DIDN'T MEAN TO BELITTLE HER PROBLEMS, AT THE END OF THE DAY WE'VE ALL GOT OUR OWN STRUGGLES AND JUST COZ I'M TRANS IT DOESN'T MEAN I'M WORSE OFF THAN ANYONE ELSE, I SEE THAT NOW BUT IT'S TOO LATE, BUT THEN AGAIN I WONDER IF WE JUST WEREN'T EVER GONNA WORK COZ, LIKE, I WAS SO OBSESSED WITH BEING THE BEST BOYFRIEND THAT I WAS NEVER TRULY **MASELF** BUT THE ONLY REASON I WAS TRYING SO HARD IS COZ I FEEL **INADEQUATE** COZ OF MA **STUPID BODY** AND IT'S GONNA BE FOREVER TIL I GET ANY SURGERIES, BUT TBH EVEN AFTER I GET THEM WHAT IF PPL WILL ALWAYS BE FREAKED OUT BY MY PAST AND THIS IS WHY I SHOULDA **CLUNG** ON TO THE ONE PERSON WHO ACCEPTED ME COZ SHE WAS PROBS THE ONLY PERSON IN THE WORLD WHO WOULD BUT I'VE GONE AND RUINED IT, IF ONLY I WASN'T BLOODY TRANS, NO, BUT YOU DON'T **UNDERSTAND** BLAH BLAH BLAH BLAH WORDS WORDS WORDS BLA BLAHH BLA WORDS WORDS WORD

PRESS

PRESS

Ctrl Z

194

5TH JUNE 2009
DAYS ON TESTOSTERONE: 285
DAYS TIL 1ST YEAR UNI DEADLINES: 18

Manchester Univ

LGBT+

MY PREVIOUS EXPERIENCE WITH **THERAPY** HADN'T BEEN SO POSITIVE BUT AT THIS POINT I HAD NOTHING TO LOSE. I TOOK A CHANCE ON A UNI COUNSELLOR.

ENTER THERAPY SESH ▶

THANKFULLY, THIS TIME I'D FOUND A THERAPIST I ACTUALLY **CONNECTED** WITH.

LET'S TACKLE **ONE** THING AT A TIME HERE.

I GET THAT A LOT...

YOU SAY THERE'S ALL THESE **EXPECTATIONS** AS A MAN...

BUT WHO FROM?

I DUNNO... EVERYONE... THE **WORLD**... MAYBE MAINLY... **ME?**

WHAT WOULD IT FEEL LIKE TO **LET GO** OF ALL THESE **EXPECTATIONS?** FOCUS ON YOUR-SELF AS A **PERSON** RATHER THAN A **PERSONA?**

PERSONA...

WHAT DO YOU MEAN, PERSONA?

I JUST MEAN WHAT IF YOU CONCENTRATE ON DOING THINGS THAT MAKE YOU **HAPPY**, AS OPPOSED TO DOING THINGS TO TRY TO **CONTROL** HOW OTHERS **SEE** YOU.

I WASN'T QUITE READY TO FULLY LET GO OF THE PERSONA YET.

I'VE WORKED SO HARD FOR SO LONG ON TRYING TO GET EVERYONE TO SEE ME AS A REGULAR GUY...

IT'D BE SCARY TO GIVE THAT UP!

I MEAN, THERE ARE PEOPLE I CAN BE TOTALLY MYSELF AROUND...

MA MUM, MA MATES LIKE MELKA AND JESS...

ARE ANY OF YOUR FRIENDS ON THE SAME JOURNEY AS YOU?

NO... I DON'T KNOW ANYONE WHO IS.

HOW DOES THAT FEEL?

SOMETIMES A BIT LONELY, HONESTLY.

AT THE END OF OUR SESSION, THE COUNSELOR GAVE ME A SUGGESTION.

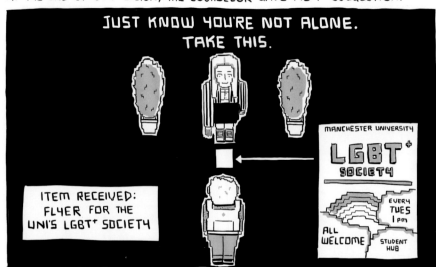

JUST KNOW YOU'RE NOT ALONE. TAKE THIS.

MANCHESTER UNIVERSITY

LGBT+ SOCIETY

EVERY TUES 1 PM

ALL WELCOME

STUDENT HUB

ITEM RECEIVED: FLYER FOR THE UNI'S LGBT+ SOCIETY

ON MY WAY BACK TO HALLS I REFLECTED...

I SET MY EXPECTATIONS SUPER HIGH (AS ALWAYS) FOR THE <u>LGBT+</u> MEETUP:

THE **REALITY** WAS, I HAD NO IDEA IF ANYONE THERE WAS LIKE ME OR NOT! PLUS, ANY NEW GROUP OF PEOPLE BROUGHT ON MY SOCIAL **ANXIETY.**

EVEN WITH LGBT PEOPLE I WAS RELUCTANT TO TELL ANYONE I WAS TRANS.

I HAD A BLAST... BUT IT WASN'T THE SUPPORT I WAS LOOKING FOR.

LIKE MANY THINGS IN MY LIFE, I GAVE UP AFTER ONE GO... BEFORE I HAD A CHANCE TO LEARN THAT THIS GUY WAS TRANS TOO!

WHILE I HID MY HISTORY IN MOST OF MY REAL LIFE, I WAS ACTUALLY PUTTING SHORT EDITS OF MY VIDEO PORTRAIT UP ON YOUTUBE.

YOUTUBE HAD A DIFFERENT VIBE BACK IN 2009. IT WAS EASY TO STAY PRETTY ANONYMOUS.

MR LEWZER'S CHANNEL

Style: Vlogging   Subscribers: 3

Just documenting my transition from female to male.

290 DAYS ON TESTOSTERONE

YOU COULD COUNT ALL THE TRANS VLOGGERS ON TWO HANDS AND THEY WERE ALL AMERICAN.

FUN FACT: THE OLD DAYS HAD A STAR RATING SYSTEM.

MR LEWZER

25 views

Comments (4):

MY ONLY INTERACTIONS WERE FROM OTHER UK TRANS PEOPLE WHO FELT ALONE LIKE ME.

Suggested Videos:

FEMALE TO MALE

Transman 1983_ USA

POST OP RECOVERY

Ftm JakesJourney_to_Joy_

TRANSITION TIMELINE

IT FELT MORE VALIDATING BEING SUPPORTED BY TOTAL STRANGERS...

Comments (4):

 Paul! at the Disco 1992:

You're looking so much more masculine now mate, I'm jealous !!!

 Sarah Soon Sam:

I start my hormones next month and this is so inspiring to see x

 Going Thru Changes 76:

I'm MtF (male to female) and love seeing how the other side live.

BUT I WASN'T PREPARED FOR THE TROLLS.

 User 809324590073987763:

ur not a real man lol

I WAS SURE I COULD PERSUADE THIS RANDOM PERSON TO UNDERSTAND.

TAP TAP TAP TAP TAP TAP TAP

MRLEWZER:

You don't understand, yes I was born female but I've felt male inside my whole life, I just knew my body should be a guy's, and now I live my life just like any other man, you wouldn't even know I was trans if you met me on the street so you wouldn't be saying what you're saying, I don't think it's right to put someone down when you have no idea what they've been through, hope this helps you understand a bit more.

MY PASSIONATE REPLY WAS MET WITH THIS THOUGHTFUL RESPONSE:

LEVEL FOUR
SELF-
ACCEPTANCE

CONTINUE

I WASN'T EVEN REALLY SURE HOW TO SHAVE. I'D NEVER BEEN TAUGHT!

IN AN IDEAL WORLD (I.E. IF I GREW UP A BOY):

VS. REALITY:

IT WAS A BIG DAY AT UNI: THE CLASS SCREENING OF OUR VIDEO PORTRAITS.

THE OTHERS' FILMS DIDN'T SEEM ANYWHERE NEAR AS **PERSONAL** AS MINE...

WHILE SOME ASPECTS OF MY LIFE WERE PROGRESSING, MY SELF-SABOTAGING WAS MAKING ME QUESTION IF UNI WAS RIGHT FOR ME.

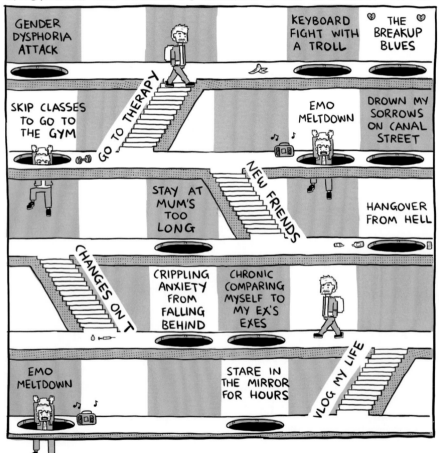

I SNUCK BACK TO MY ROOM AND LOOKED AT ALL OF THE PILING ASSIGNMENTS.

AT THIS POINT I FELT TOO FAR BEHIND TO EVER RECOVER.

THE FACT IT FELT LIKE A RELIEF TOLD ME SOMETHING.

I WAS STARTING TO REALIZE IT DIDN'T MATTER **WHERE** I LIVED... THE REAL "**HELL**" I'D BEEN TRYING TO ESCAPE WAS MY **OWN HEAD**!

I KNEW DROPPING OUT WASN'T GONNA BE EASY. MUM WOULD HIT THE ROOF. BUT I USED IT AS MOTIVATION TO FIND A PURPOSE BACK HOME.

THE JOB AT MY OLD GYM ENTICED ME. I WAS SURE I'D FEEL LIKE A "REAL BIG MAN" WORKING AROUND BODYBUILDERS. I GOT A PHONE INTERVIEW.

IGNORING THE FACT THAT THE GYM SEEMED SUSPICIOUSLY DESPERATE TO HIRE SOMEONE, I WAS *BUZZIN'* FOR THIS NEW LIFE PATH.

I WAS SAD TO LEAVE MELKA, THOUGH.

AS I LEFT THE CITY, I BROKE THE BIG NEWS TO MUM.

I SWEAR MUM TOOK THE NEWS WORSE THAN WHEN I CAME OUT AS TRANS! I ARRIVED HOME TO THIS...

ME AND **GRANDMA** ALWAYS HAD A **SPECIAL** KINDA CLOSENESS.

I'D WORKED OUT AT THIS GYM LOADS BUT I WAS DEAD NERVOUS TO WORK HERE - I'D ACTUALLY HAVE TO INTERACT WITH PEOPLE!

YES, THE GYM REALLY DID HAVE A BAR! I SWEAR ALL THIS WASN'T PART OF THE JOB DESCRIPTION...

THINGS GOT TOO HOT TO HANDLE IN MY **BINDER** UNDER MY SHIRT.

AFTER A FEW SHIFTS, I THINK THE STRANGE LOCALS GREW TO LIKE ME.

ME **EX-WIFE** WON'T *SNIFF* TALK TO ME NO MORE *SNORT* WHAT DO I **DO**, **NEW BOY**? OHHH NOOO...

ANOTHER ONE O' ME "SUZIE **SPECIALS**", DUCK.

DON'T FORGET ME SPECIAL GLASS.

I USED TO BE REAL BUFF, ATE A **PIG'S HEART** EVERY DAY.

NONE OF THEM HAD EVEN THE SLIGHTEST **INKLING** THAT I WAS TRANS.

ONE TIME:

NEW BOY! I NIPPED TO THE BUTCHER'S, YOU'RE TOO PUNY, NEED TO BEEF UP.

DON'T BE A **GIRL**. OPEN IT UP! S'ONLY AN **ORGAN**.

OH GOD.

OK, THANKS, HEH.

THEY UNKNOWINGLY GAVE ME A GIFT. MY FIRST REAL EXPERIENCE OF:

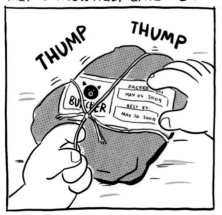

THUMP THUMP

PACKED ON MAY 04 2009

BEST BY: MAY 20 2009

BUTCHER

STEALTH LIFE

REAL MAN

224

A FEW OF THEIR COMMENTS WOULD WIND ME UP. I WONDERED HOW THEY'D REACT TO ME IF MY SECRET SPRUNG OUT THE BOX.

MUM CAME TO ACCEPT MY DECISION TO LEAVE UNI. SHE WAS HAPPY TO SEE ME STICKING THIS JOB OUT.

THE NEXT LEVEL OF MY TRANSITION WAS FINALLY IN REACH!

GOD, IT FELT SO INVASIVE.

EVERYTHING FELT HOPELESS.

THE HEALTH CARE SYSTEM WAS SET UP ALL **WRONG** FOR **TRANS MEN** IN MY HOMETOWN BACK THEN. CHEST SURGERY IS NORMALLY THE **FIRST** SURGICAL STEP. NOT EVERY-BODY WANTS THE **LOWER** SURGERY.

IN FACT, EVERY SINGLE TRANS-ITION IS **UNIQUE**. THERE ISN'T **ONE WAY** TO BE TRANS.

ST. HELL HAS CAUGHT UP **NOW**, THANKFULLY. BUT 20-YR-OLD ME WAS DEVASTATED.

I HAD ANOTHER PHONE CONFESSIONAL WITH JESS.

I COULDN'T JUST PRETEND EVERYTHING WAS FINE IN FRONT OF ALL THE GYM BROS AND DRUNKS AT WORK.

MY MATE LAURA SHOWED UP, TRYING TO GET ME OUTA MY FUNK.

AS LUCK WOULD BLOODY HAVE IT...

ANXIETY

HIYA, I CAN EXPLAIN, I'M—

FIRED !!!!!

EVERY LAST SHRED OF MY MAN POINTS GONE.

REAL MAN

ZOOOM

−1 GYM JOB

MY OLD SALES ASSISTANT JOB

THE INK PAD arts & crafts

JOB VACANCY

SALE

OPEN

THANKFULLY THE ART SHOP ACCEPTED ME BACK WITH OPEN ARMS. AT LEAST I COULD ALWAYS BE MYSELF THERE.

SNIFF AND THE SURGEON SAID I'M NOT A MAN *SNIFF* BUT THEY DON'T UNDERSTAND *CRY*

BOSS: MARION

THERE, THERE, DARLIN'. I'LL MAKE US A BREW.

← MY "WORK MUM"

0.00

233

IT WAS LIKE I'D RETURNED TO MY LAST "SAVE POINT" IN LIFE™.

♪ AND ALL MY MATES ARE DWINDLING DOWN ♪♪

ALISON WAS STILL AT UNI IN LONDON.

JESS MOVED OUTA TOWN TO BE CLOSER TO WORK.

www.facebook.com

Alison is in a relationship. **f**

👍 95 like this.

www.facebook.com

Jess just got promoted to shift manager at work omg #bossbitch 🍾🍾 **f**

♪♪ FEELS LIKE EVERYONE'S LEVELLING UP THEIR LIVES, WHILE I'M STILL HERE STRIVIN' TO SURVIVE ♪♪

HELLO, THE INK PAD ARTS AND CRAFTS, YOUR NUMBER ONE SHOP FOR BITS N' BOBS.

10% OFF

GALLERY UPSTAIRS

ST. HELL ART SHOW

SKETCHBOOKS HALF PRICE

I CALCULATED ROUGHLY HOW LONG IT'D TAKE TO SAVE FOR SURGERY IF I WERE TO GO DOWN THE **PRIVATE** HEALTH CARE ROUTE.

I TRIED MY LUCK WITH THE BANK OF MUM...

BUT IT WAS OUT OF **FUNDS.**

238

BUT YOU **KNEW** I'D ALWAYS FELT LIKE A BOY, RIGHT?

YES, BUT WHEN YOU CAME OUT AS A **LESBIAN** FIRST, I FELT RELIEVED 'COS I THOUGHT YOU'D FINALLY FOUND A WAY TO BE **HAPPY**...

A LIFE THAT DIDN'T INVOLVE SUCH **INVASIVE** PROCEDURES.

THE TABLES TURNED. I TRIED SUPPORTING MUM FOR A CHANGE.

WOULD IT HELP YOU TO WATCH SOME VIDEOS OF **OTHER** TRANS PEOPLE ON YOUTUBE WHO'VE HAD SURGERIES?

IT MIGHT, ACTUALLY

IT'D BE GOOD TO NOT FEEL LIKE THE ONLY ONES IN THE **WORLD** GOING THROUGH THIS.

ADULT CHAT WITH MUM

REAL MAN

241

I HAD TO GET **CREATIVE** WITH EARNING MONEY FOR SURGERY. I SCOURED ST. HELL FOR OPPORTUNITIES...

AND TOOK A RISK.

HIYA, I'M A, ERM, SORT OF A FILMMAKER?

NICE ONE. WE WANT A SHORT FILM MADE THAT INSPIRES THE YOUTH IN THIS TOWN TO GET WORKING.

WE CAN PAY YOU £250, CASH IN HAND.

I GOT **MELKA** TO VISIT. LITTLE DID SHE KNOW I HAD A **ROLE** FOR HER...

THEY JUST WANTED BASIC INTERVIEWS WITH DIFFERENT KINDSA WORKERS ROUND TOWN...

BUT I THOUGHT THAT SOUNDED BORRRING SO...

THE THINGS I DO FOR YOU...

PROPS

IT WAS FUN TO FLEX MY FILMMAKING SKILLS AGAIN!

WE WERE ONE SHOT AWAY FROM FINISHING WHEN MELKA TWISTED HER ANKLE.

IT WAS LIKE I EXPECTED TO TURN BACK INTO MY FEMALE SELF...

BUT I DIDN'T. (SHOCKING, I KNOW.) BENEATH THE COSTUME, I WAS STILL ME.

THE THING ABOUT IDENTITY IS IT'S NOT YOUR CLOTHES, IT'S WHO YOU ARE.

IT SEEMED I WAS STARTING TO FEEL MORE SECURE IN MY MANHOOD.

THE YOUTH GROUP WORKERS ARRANGED A "SK8 GRAN" SCREENING IN TOWN.

I INVITED EVERYONE FOR MORAL SUPPORT. (WELL, NEARLY EVERYONE.)

I WAS PROPER CHUFFED WITH THE AUDIENCE'S REACTION!

IT WAS AWESOME TO BE CELEBRATED FOR MY CREATIVITY...

AND MADE ME FEEL BETTER ABOUT QUITTING UNI. LIKE I WAS FORGING MY OWN PATH, IN MY OWN TIME.

MAYBE I DID HAVE A HABIT OF PAINTING DAD AS THE BAD GUY...

THE FILM NIGHT GAVE ME A CONFIDENCE BOOST AND INSPIRED ME TO KEEP GOING! I BEGAN MAKING ALL KINDS OF SILLY (CRINGEY) VIDEOS.

IT FELT DEAD GOOD TO BE EXCITED ABOUT STUFF. BEFORE I KNEW IT, I WAS HAVING FUN WITHOUT EVEN **THINKING** ABOUT BEING TRANS.

I WAS DUE A FINAL SESSION WITH MY THERAPIST THROUGH UNI. I WAS EAGER TO TELL HER HOW WELL I'D BEEN DOING LATELY.

ENTER THERAPY SESH ▶

HOW HAVE YOU BEEN, LEWIS?

GOOD, ACTUALLY! I THINK I'VE STARTED TO LET GO OF SOME OF THE IDEAS I HAD ABOUT WHO I SHOULD BE...

LIKE, I USED TO THINK I HAD TO HAVE ALL MALE MATES TO BE SEEN AS "ONE OF THE GUYS"...

C'MON! LADS!

LADS!

LADS!

SPORTY

BUT NOW I REALIZE IT'S ABOUT WHO MAKES ME HAPPY AS A FRIEND... AND MOST OF MY MATES ARE GIRLS ANYWAY!

YOU'RE SO SOFT, LEW.

SNIFF I CAN'T BELIEVE SHANE AND CARMEN BROKE UP! *SNIFF*

(YEAH, I CAN CRY AGAIN NOW.)

POPCORN

HOT TORTILLAS

the L word

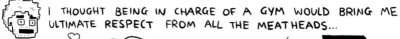 I THOUGHT BEING IN CHARGE OF A GYM WOULD BRING ME ULTIMATE RESPECT FROM ALL THE MEATHEADS...

BUT GETTING FIRED WAS A BLESSING IN DISGUISE COS NOW I'M BACK TO MY **CREATIVE SELF** AND LOOKING INTO **FILM** OPPORTUNITIES AGAIN!

AND I'M NOT AS CAUGHT UP IN HAVING THIS **SHREDDED** PHYSIQUE ANYMORE. I'M STARTING TO KINDA LIKE MY REFLECTION!

IT SOUNDS LIKE YOU'VE BEEN DOING SOME REALLY GREAT WORK ON YOURSELF.

SO HOW ARE YOU FEELING ABOUT THE FUTURE?

REALLY HOPEFUL! I'VE STARTED SAVING FOR MY CHEST SURGERY! KNOWING I'M A LIL' CLOSER TO THAT MAKES ME RELAX A BIT.

AND I DECIDED TO EASE UP ON MY FOOD AND GYM PLAN TO SEE WHERE TESTOSTERONE NATURALLY TAKES MY BODY.

WHICH GIVES ME SPACE FOR OTHER LIFE STUFF.

I'VE REACHED A POINT NOW WHERE I JUST DON'T THINK OF MYSELF AS TRANS!

I MEAN, I PROBABLY SHOULDN'T RELAX TOO MUCH, THOUGH...

THIS PHYSICAL STATE I'M IN IS COOL FOR NOW BUT NOT FOREVER...

IMAGINE IF I GET NO MORE CHANGES ON HORMONES...

OR IF MY SURGERY DOESN'T EVEN HAPPEN !!!

AND I'VE LET MASELF GO ALL FOR NOTHING !!!

WHAT IF I'M PAUSING MY TRANSITION BY PAUSING MY WORRYING ABOUT IT????

OH GOD, NOW I'M SCARED !!!

DID YOU NOTICE YOUR THOUGHT PATTERN TURNS YOUR POSITIVES INTO NEGATIVES WHEN YOU TALK ABOUT RELAXING?

(GOOD THING + GOOD THING) x RELAXING = BAD THING

WHAT IS IT ABOUT RELAXING THAT WORRIES YOU?

I GUESS IT'S LIKE IF I TAKE THE PRESSURE OFF MYSELF I'M AFRAID EVERYTHING WILL GO TO SHIT.

OBSESSING HAS ALWAYS BEEN HOW I'VE ACHIEVED THINGS!

BUT MA MATES TELL ME I TRY TO CONTROL THINGS TOO MUCH!

THERE'S A DIFFERENCE BETWEEN BEING PASSIONATE ABOUT SOMETHING VERSUS OBSESSIVELY WORRYING.

WORRYING CAN'T CHANGE THE OUTCOME OF A SITUATION.

IT WILL ONLY MAKE IT LESS ENJOYABLE FOR YOU.

TO BE FAIR, LOOKING BACK, THE STUFF I'VE WORRIED ABOUT WOULD HAVE HAD THE SAME OUTCOME EITHER WAY...

SO YEAH, IT WOULD FEEL NICE TO LET MASELF, LIKE, BREATHE MORE.

A FEW MONTHS LATER:

GOAL: £6000
FUNDS: £705.95p

QUEST FOR THE CHEST

JESS AND ALISON WERE KEEN TO HELP ME ON MY QUEST. THEY CAME BACK TO VISIT. I FELT NERVOUS TO SEE THEM AFTER ALL THIS TIME.

THEY SEEMED MORE CONCERNED ABOUT THEIR OWN CHANGES!

THE OLD GANG WAS BACK TOGETHER. WE STARTED SCHEMING...

WE CELEBRATED OUR PLAN WITH THE STANDARD ST. HELL SCRAN.

MUM SUGGESTED I ASK **DAD** TO HELP WITH ORGANIZING THE FUND-RAISER SINCE SINCE HE USED TO PUT ON KARAOKE NIGHTS.

Hellhole
Inn ~
PUB
LUNCH
CHEAP
BEER

THAT MUST BE DAD'S NEW GIRLFRIEND!

HOW'S HE GONNA GENDER ME IN FRONT OF HER?

THIS COULD GET AWKWARD...

VICKY, MEET OUR **LOIS** - I MEAN - OUR **LEWIS.**

GOOD TO SEE HIM TRYING!

NICE TO MEET YA.

YOU TOO!

DAD AND I HADN'T ACTUALLY TALKED ABOUT THINGS IN DETAIL...

'AV GOTTA SAY, I DON'T GET WHY YA WANT THIS SURGERY...

NEIL —

NO, VICKY, 'AV GOTTA TALK TO HER — —HIM— ABOUT IT.

D'YA NOT THINK YER BEIN' TOO PICKY?

YA LOOK AL'REET TO ME.

I FIGURED HE JUST NEEDED TO HEAR IT IN HIS OWN LANGUAGE.

I WAS PSYCHED FOR THE BIG NIGHT. I WONDERED HOW MANY PEOPLE WOULD SHOW AND HOPED THEY'D ALL ENJOY IT!

THE ACTUAL FLYERS I STUCK UP ALL AROUND TOWN

I WAS SHOOK BY SUCH A BIG TURNOUT, WHICH INCLUDED A SUPRISING AMOUNT OF RANDOMS, THANKS TO JESS!

I PROBABLY SHOULD HAVE SPECIFIED WHAT "QUEST FOR THE "CHEST" MEANT ON THE FLYERS...

MY VOICE LITERALLY TREMBLED AS I ADDRESSED THE ROOM...

I TRIED NOT TO FOCUS ON THE STRANGERS...

INSTEAD I LOOKED AT ALL THE PEOPLE FROM MY LIFE WHO HAD COME TOGETHER TO SUPPORT MY TRANSITION. I FELT SO LUCKY.

TURNS OUT SPEAKING IT OUT LOUD WASN'T THE END OF THE WORLD! ONCE I GOT GOING, I JUST SPOKE FROM THE HEART.

AS MOST OF YOU KNOW... I'M TRANSGENDER.

I'M FUNDRAISING FOR SURGERY TO GET, ERM, A MALE CHEST, COZ THE LOCAL NHS HAVE DENIED ME.

BUT THIS SURGERY IS LIFE SAVING TO ME.

SO, LIKE, I JUST CAN'T THANK YOU ALL ENOUGH FOR BEING HERE, LIKE.

NO WAY! *GASP* AWWW! WOO!

THE REST OF THE NIGHT WENT LIKE:

ME, MELKA, AND LAURA PERFORMING MY CRINGEY SONGS.

OMG, MY EX RAE IS HERE!

THE PAST IS THE PAST. I KNOW HOW MUCH THIS SURGERY MEANS TO HIM.

ALISON AND JESS COLLECTING DONATIONS.

BAR

CHEERS!

MUM WORKING THE DOOR.

TWO POUND ENTRY, LOVE.

QUEST FOR THE CHEST

DAD AND MUM'S BOYFRIEND ARE OLD BANDMATES. NEVER THOUGHT I'D SEE THEM GET ON AGAIN!

DAD CLOSED THE EVENING WITH A SONG, BUT NOT BEFORE SAYING:

IT FELT LIKE WE'D ALL ACCOMPLISHED SOMETHING TOGETHER.

A FEW WEEKS LATER, THE MOST **INSANE** THING HAPPENED...

NEW EMAIL

MY LITTLE **YOUTUBE** CHANNEL GOT **NOTICED** BY A **TV** COMPANY!

www.gmail.com/inbox

Subject : Tv show   From : casting @ productioncompany

Dear Lewis,

We love your videos on YouTube!

We are a production company developing a documentary TV series for a major broadcaster.

The show would follow seven transgender people's lives with the intention of educating the public on the issues you face in a fun, entertaining, and sensitive way.

Would you be interested in taking part?

All the best,

TV series   transgender people's lives

major broadcaster.

I STARTED TO THINK ABOUT MY YOUNGER SELF AND WHETHER THIS SHOW WOULD HAVE HELPED.

SNIFF *CRY* I DON'T WANNA FEEL LIKE A BOY. I WANNA FEEL LIKE A GIRL. I'M SUPPOSED TO BE A GIRL.

HEY, FOURTEEN-YEAR-OLD ME... WHAT IF YOU GOT TO SEE THERE ARE OTHER PEOPLE LIKE YOU? THAT IT'S TOTALLY POSSIBLE TO GROW UP TO BE A MAN... AND LIVE A HAPPY LIFE...?

HOW WOULD YOU FEEL?

DUNNO...

HOPEFUL.

I KNEW THEN I HAD TO DO IT...

FOR LOIS.

UNDERNEATH THE WORRIES, I FELT THIS FIRE INSIDE ME THAT WANTED
TO HELP OTHERS BY PUTTING MY TRUE SELF OUT THERE.

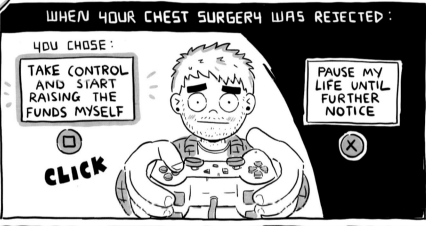

1ST JULY 2010
AGE: 21
DAYS ON
TESTOSTERONE: 671
DAYS TIL THE SHOW
STARTS FILMING: 0

THE SHOW FILMED AT A MAJESTIC OLD MILL HOUSE. I'D BE SPENDING THE SUMMER WEEKENDS HERE ALONG WITH THE REST OF THE CAST.

AS I GOT OUT THE TAXI, I QUESTIONED IF I'D DONE THE RIGHT THING...

OK, WHY DID IT FEEL LIKE I'D KNOWN THESE TWO FOREVER?

IT WAS LIBERATING TO BE AROUND OTHERS ON THE SAME JOURNEY AS ME!

WE ALL JUST GOT EACH OTHER.

WE BECAME LIKE A PROPER LIL FAMILY IN THAT HOUSE.

FULL DISCLOSURE, I MAY HAVE DEVELOPED A LIL' CRUSH IN THE HOUSE...

THAT WAS A POSITION I NEVER PREDICTED I'D BE IN! IT GAVE ME SOME EMPATHY WITH THE GIRLS WHO DATE ME...

I SOON GOT USED TO BEING IN THE HOT SEAT. I KINDA THRIVED OFF IT!

AND I PUT MY KNACK OF ASKING QUESTIONS TO GOOD USE FOR ONCE (I THINK THE CREW FELT LIKE THE ONES BEING INTERVIEWED!)

THE BEST MOMENTS HAPPENED WHEN THE CAMERAS **WEREN'T** ROLLING.

I LEARNED IT'S OK TO **SLIP UP**, IT'S WHAT YOU DO AFTERWARDS THAT COUNTS!

A FEW WEEKS LATER, THE TV SHOW AIRED. A BUNCH OF US EXCITEDLY HUDDLED AROUND THE TELLY IN MUM'S LIVING ROOM TO WATCH.

PEOPLE REALLY DID WATCH IT! AND ST.HELL PROVED TO NOT BE SO SMALL-MINDED AFTER ALL.

Hopefully make **allies** from the general public

WELL DONE, MATE!

'ERE, IT'S THAT LAD OFF THE TELLY!

RANDOM TOWNIES

REPPIN' ST.HELL!

BARGAIN BO[O]

MY FIRST TIME BACK TO THE GYM SINCE THE SHOW (AND BEING FIRED):

BLIMEY, I'D NEVER HAVE KNOWN, LOVEY.

GOBSMACKED, I WAS.

THE LOCALS

I NEVER EVEN KNEW A WOMAN TO MAN EXISTED!

A chance to dispel myths about trans ppl!

I GUESS WE'RE ALL GUILTY OF MAKING PREJUDGMENTS SOMETIMES!

NICE ONE, BRO. ME N' MY BOYFRIEND WATCHED YOUR SHOW.

"BOYFRIEND"??! WAIT, WHY AM I GOBSMACKED?

GYM BRO

SPORTY

ON THE ODD NIGHT OUT I HAD TO DEAL WITH SOME OF THE 'CONS'...

RIGHTLY OR WRONGLY, I STAYED MY OVERLY POLITE, OVERSHARING SELF.

I REALIZED PEOPLE'S INTENTIONS WERE USUALLY IN THE RIGHT PLACE.

MUM STRUGGLED TO BRUSH OFF ANY ONLINE HATE THAT THE SHOW ATTRACTED. AS MUCH AS I LOVED HOW **PROUD** SHE WAS OF ME, IT DEFINITELY **GOT** TO HER A BIT TOO MUCH.

287

I GOT AN INTERESTING CALL FROM JESS ONE TIME...

OMG, LEW, GUESS WHO I'VE JUST BUMPED INTO...

I'll cringe if ppl from high school watch it

OH GOD, GO ON...

THE TRENDIES!! THEY ALL SAW YOU ON TV AND SAY YOU LOOK FIT NOW!

TELL HIM TO SEND US AN ADDY ON FACEYB!

WHAT!!

NOT GONNA LIE, THE LOIS IN ME LOVED TO HEAR IT. IT DEFO HELPED SOME OF THE ANXIOUS THOUGHTS MELT AWAY.

GAABLEUGHACKLOPPUHU

ME AND FOX FROM THE SHOW DECIDED TO START TELLING OTHER TRANS PEOPLE'S STORIES IN AN **AUTHENTIC** WAY.

THIS LED TO US SETTING UP OUR ONGOING FILM PROJECT:

FOX LIVED DOWN SOUTH IN BRIGHTON. I ENDED UP SPENDING A BIT OF TIME THERE THROUGH OUR PROJECTS. (MELKA CAME TOO!)

THE SHOW HAD CAPTURED MORE OF MY QUEST FOR THE CHEST.

DREW AND DONNA PERFORMING AT ONE OF MY LOCAL FUNDRAISERS. (ST.HELL LOVED IT.)

DM FROM A SUPPORTIVE VIEWER

Hey, I'd love to come to your next fundraiser but I can't make it. Can you set up a GoFundMe so people who can't come can still donate?

SO I SET UP A GOFUNDME ACCOUNT THAT WENT KINDA VIRAL...

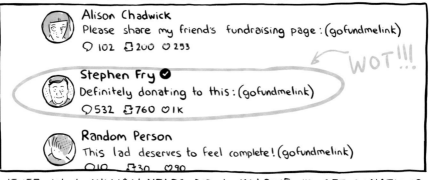

Alison Chadwick
Please share my friend's fundraising page: (gofundmelink)
♡ 102 🔁 200 ♡ 253

Stephen Fry ✓
Definitely donating to this: (gofundmelink)
♡ 532 🔁 760 ♡ 1K

WOT!!!

Random Person
This lad deserves to feel complete! (gofundmelink)
♡ 10 🔁 30 ♡ 90

NEVER IN A MILLION YEARS DID I IMAGINE I'D GET DONATIONS FROM PEOPLE ALL OVER THE COUNTRY! I WAS BLOWN AWAY.

OMG!!! MUM, COME LOOK!!!

👍 Might lead to help with my chest surgery

gofundme
£3,500 of £4K goal
QUEST FOR THE

291

I BOOKED MY SURGERY WITH A RENOWNED GENDER SURGEON IN BRIGHTON. MUM AND DAD TOOK ME DOWN THERE TO THE HOSPITAL.

AS MUCH AS MY JOURNEY FELT LIKE A NEVER-ENDING HELL...

I CAN'T DENY IT GAVE ME THE TIME TO FIGURE MYSELF OUT.

IT WAS ALL WORTH THE WAIT.   MY FUTURE FINALLY LOOKED...

MY EXCITEMENT WAS OVERIDDEN BY MAJOR ANXIETY ABOUT GOING UNDER. THIS WAS A BIG OPERATION, AFTER ALL.

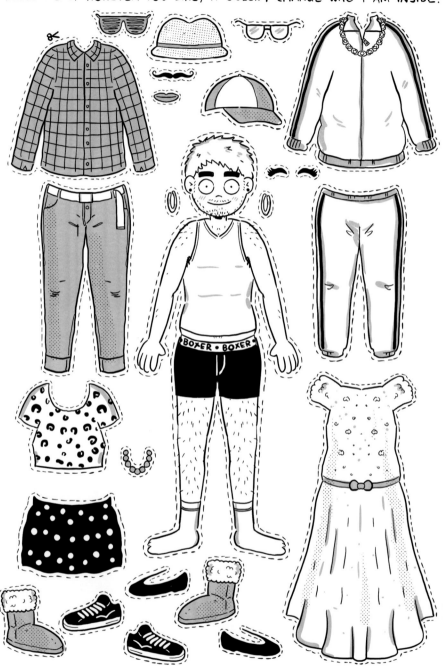

THERE'S INFINITE WAYS I CAN EXPRESS MYSELF AS A MAN.

HOW DO MEN HANDLE THEIR EMOTIONS?

	CRY	TALK TO MATES	FEEL THE FEELINGS
	WRITE IT DOWN	MAKE A VLOG	
GO TO THERAPY		SING A SONG	
	BLAST EMO TUNES	TALK TO FAMILY	SET HEALTHY BOUNDARIES
WRITE A BOOK	LET IT GO		BREATHE
	DANCE	PLAY GAMES	
	MAKE ART	OPEN UP TO MY PARTNER	CUDDLE A CAT
MAKE A FILM		TALK TO MYSELF	FORGIVE MYSELF
	TAKE TIME OUT	BE VULNERABLE	SCREAM INTO A PILLOW
HAVE A SELF-CARE DAY			GO FOR A SKATE
WATCH A FUNNY VIDEO		HAVE AN INTERNET DETOX	
			NAP
			EAT
WORK OUT			MEDITATE
			GO FOR A WALK
TEXT A MATE			TIDY MY ROOM
			LAUGH IT OFF
BINGE WATCH MY COMFORT TV SHOW		TRY A NEW HOBBY	
			RUN TO MUM

THERE'S NO WINNING IF I TREAT RELATIONSHIPS LIKE EXPERIMENTS.

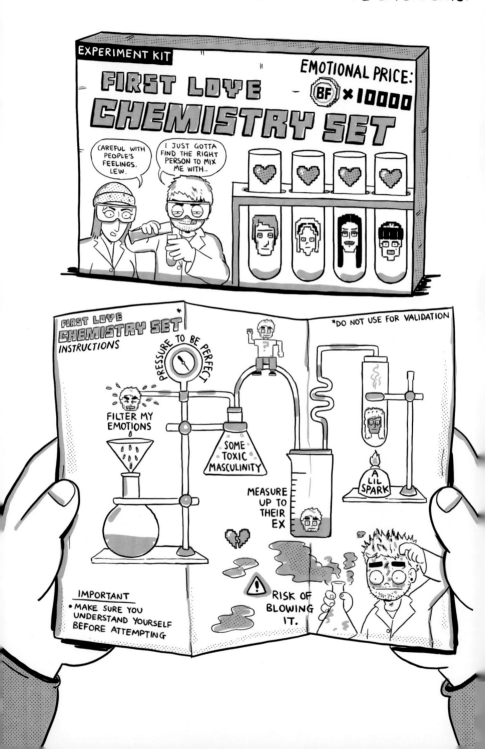

IF LIFE IS A GAME, I WANNA PLAY IT AS THE REAL ME.

STUPENDOUS BOY
EPISODE 1:
QUEST FOR THE CHEST!

FUNDRAISING
PARTY
FOR LEWIS HANCOX

LIVE ENTERTAINMENT . ACOUSTIC SETS . RAFFLE
ARTWORK . DJ . LOTS OF BOOZE!

£2 BAR JAVA ST HELENS

(THIS EVENT WILL BE FILMED BY TWENTY TWENTY TELEVISION FOR POSSIBLE
INCLUSION IN A MAJOR DOCUMENTARY TO BE AIRED LATER THIS YEAR.)

ME JESS ALISON

AGE 19

INTRODUCING MELKA AS: SK8 GRAN

A FILM BY LEWIS HANCOX

MELKA N' ME

ME N' LAURA

MUSIC IN MUM'S BATHROOM

MY GENDERATION
A new project by Fox and Lewis

ME AND FOX ON THE LAKE BOAT

MY TRANS SUMMER   2011

7 WEEKS ON T